NEIGHBORHOOD HELPERS

Nurses

BY CECILIA MINDEN AND
LINDA M. ARMANTROUT

The Child's World

Content Adviser:
Patricia Rowell, RN, PhD,
American Nurses Association,
Silver Spring, Maryland

Published in the United States of America by The Child's World®
PO Box 326
Chanhassen, MN 55317-0326
800-599-READ
www.childsworld.com

Acknowledgements

The Child's World®: Mary Berendes, Publishing Director

Editorial Directions, Inc.: E. Russell Primm, Editorial Director; Katie Marsico, Managing Editor and Line Editor; Judith Shiffer, Assistant Editor; Caroline Wood, Editorial Assistant; Susan Hindman, Copy Editor; Wendy Mead, Proofreader; Mike Helenthal, Rory Mabin, and Caroline Wood, Fact Checkers; Tim Griffin/IndexServ, Indexer; Cian Loughlin O'Day, Photo Researcher; Linda S. Koutris, Photo Selector

The Design Lab: Kathleen Petelinsek, Design and Art Production

Photographs ©: Cover: left—RubberBall Productions, right/frontispiece—Photodisc/Getty Images. Interior: 4, 17, 23—Photodisc/Getty Images; 5—RubberBall Productions; 6—Brand X Pictures; 7—R. Holz/zefa/Corbis; 8-9—Sean Justice/The Image Bank/Getty Images; 11—Bruce Ayers/Stone/ Getty Images; 13, 20-21—Gary Feinstein; 14—Phil Schermeister/Corbis; 18-19—Jim McDonald/ Corbis; 24-25—Linda M. Armantrout; 26-27—Randy Faris; 29—Cn Boon/Alamy Images.

Library of Congress Cataloging-in-Publication Data
Minden, Cecilia.
  Nurses / by Cecilia Minden and Linda M. Armantrout.
    p. cm. — (Neighborhood helpers)
  ISBN 1-59296-566-0 (library bound : alk. paper)
1. Nurses—Juvenile literature. 2. Nursing—Juvenile literature. I. Armantrout, Linda M. II. Title. III. Series.
  RT61.5.M56 2006
  610.73—dc22   2005026214

TABLE OF CONTENTS

Amber

Hello. My name is Amber. Many people live and work in my neighborhood. Each of them helps the neighborhood in different ways.

I thought of all the things I like to do. I like taking care of my friends. I like to exercise and eat healthy foods. I like to solve problems.

How could I help my neighborhood when I grow up?

Nursing as a career began in the late 1800s. The first nursing school opened in 1873 in Boston, Massachusetts.

I COULD BE A NURSE!

Nurses take care of people who are sick. They enjoy helping others.

Best of all, nurses make people feel better and teach them how to stay healthy!

Nurses teach people how to eat foods and make choices that will keep them healthy. Nurses also help people who are sick.

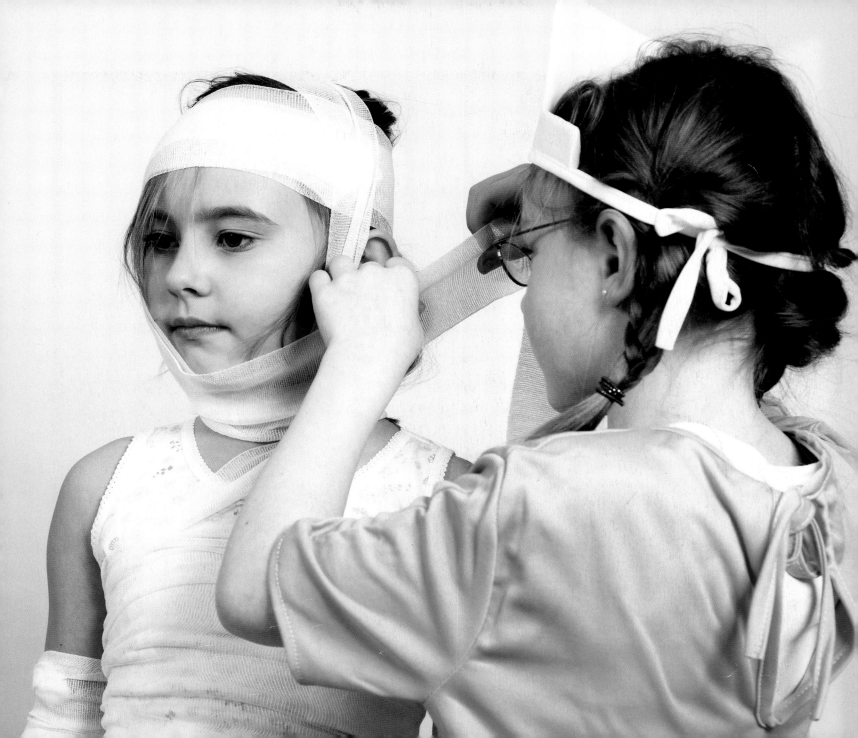

LEARN ABOUT THIS NEIGHBORHOOD HELPER!

The best way to learn is to ask questions. Words such as *who, what, where, when,* and *why* will help me learn about being a nurse.

Asking a nurse questions will help you learn more about her job.

Where Can I Learn More?

American Nurses
Association
8515 Georgia Avenue
Suite 400
Silver Spring, MD 20910

National League
for Nursing
61 Broadway, 33rd Floor
New York, NY 10006

WHO CAN BECOME A NURSE?

Boys and girls who are good at solving problems, excited about learning, and who enjoy helping others may want to become nurses. It is important for nurses to be good listeners. They must pay attention when patients tell them what is wrong.

Nurses are important to the neighborhood. They care for people who are sick. Nurses also show people things they can do to stay healthy.

Nurses need to get to know their patients. It is especially important for nurses to have good listening skills.

MEET A NURSE!

This is Mary Cordova. She is a nurse in a doctor's office in Hanford, California. She knew when she was a little girl that she wanted to be a nurse. "I really like doing what I do," says Mary. "I like that I am able to help." When Mary is not working in the doctor's office, she enjoys helping her husband remodel old cars.

Mary enjoys being a nurse because it allows her to help others.

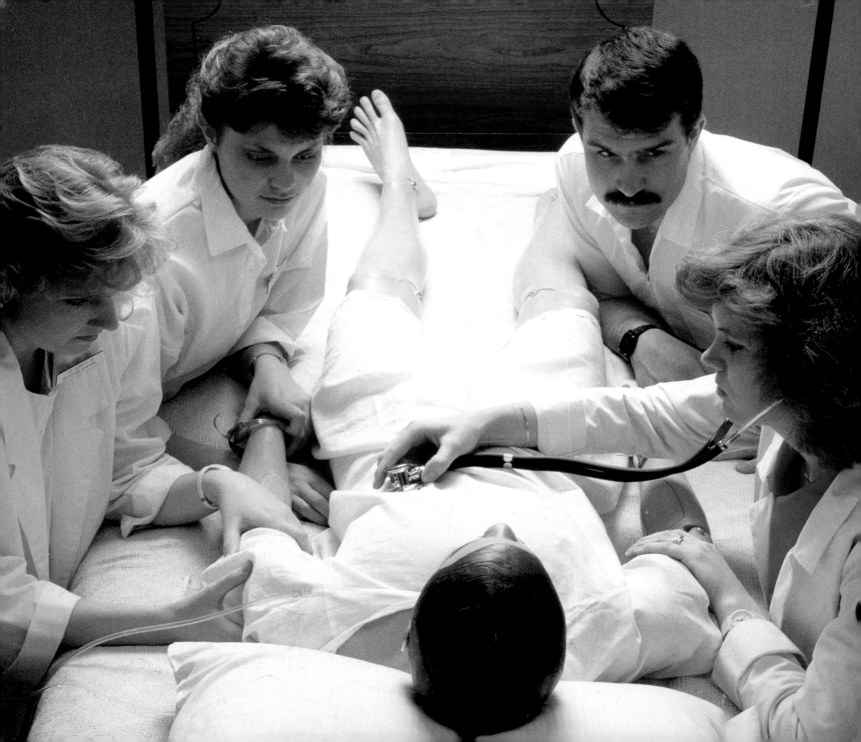

WHERE CAN I LEARN TO BE A NURSE?

People who want to become nurses must take classes in special nursing programs. There are different programs available. The programs take different amounts of time to complete.

Nurses also have to pass a test to get their nursing license. The state provides this license. The license gives a nurse permission to work.

Students in nursing school work with models. They practice how they will one day treat real patients.

How Much School Will I Need?

Many nurses have a four-year college degree. Some nurses study for two to three years at community colleges. A few nurses study for about three years in hospitals. Nurses take a test to get their license once they finish their training. A nurse with a license is called a registered nurse, or RN.

What Are Some Instruments I Will Use?

Bandages

Computer

Stethoscope

Thermometer

stethoscope (STETH-uh-skope) an instrument used to listen to sounds in a patient's heart, lungs, stomach, and other areas

WHAT DOES A NURSE NEED TO DO HER JOB?

Mary uses many different instruments to help care for patients. One important instrument is a **stethoscope.** The stethoscope helps Mary listen to the sounds inside a person's body. Everything makes a different sound. Your heart makes a *lub-dub* sound. Your stomach sometimes gurgles. It may even make a loud growl if you are really hungry!

Nurses use a stethoscope to hear the sounds inside a patient's body.

Mary often uses special words when she speaks with doctors and other nurses. Sometimes Mary needs help right away. She then asks for help "STAT!" This is short for the Latin word *statim*, which means "immediately" or "right away." Mary might use this word during an emergency, when it is important to act quickly.

What Clothes Will I Wear?

Comfortable shoes
Latex gloves
Scrubs or uniform

WHERE DOES A NURSE WORK?

Mary works in a doctor's office. Other nurses work in hospitals, factories, or schools. Many nurses are in the military. Some nurses teach classes for students who are training to be nurses. Nurses may work in different places, but they are always helping people!

Mary's job is different every day. She sees many patients who need her help. Mary uses different pieces of information to decide how to care for her patients. How fast is someone's heart beating?

Some nurses have jobs in the military.

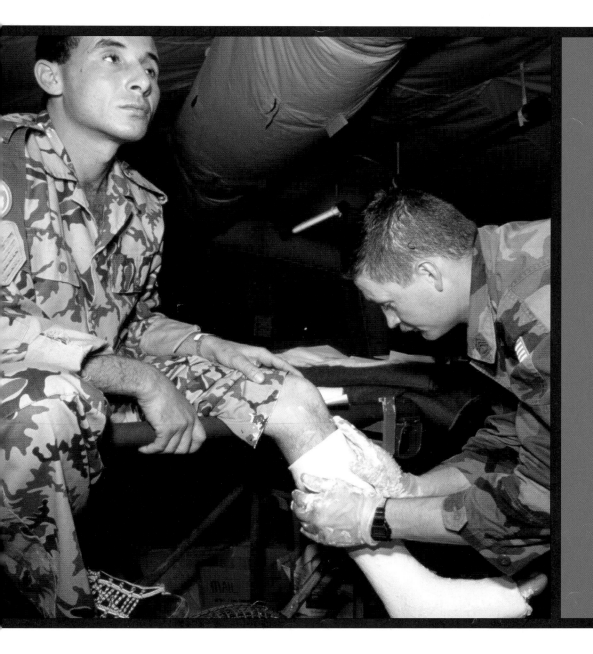

What's It Like Where I'll Work?

Hospitals and doctors' offices are very clean. They are brightly lit. Lots of people come and go. Sometimes sick people are difficult or unhappy. Nurses must always stay calm and pleasant.

How Much Money Will I Make?

Most nurses make between $34,000 and $70,000 a year.

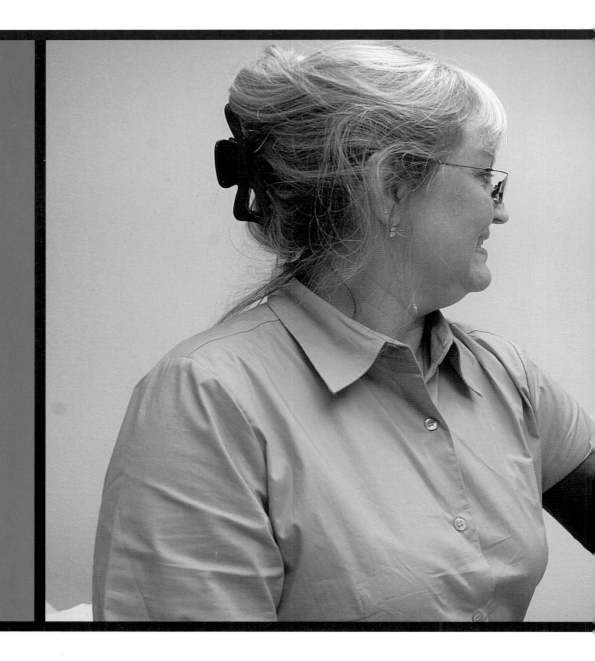

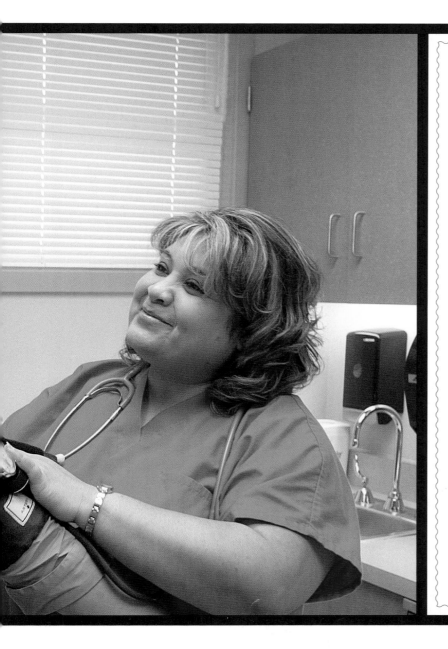

Does the person have a cut or sore? Does the patient need medicine? Is the patient sad or scared?

"I like it when patients come back and they are happy to see me," says Mary. "It's so nice to see them doing well. I try to be friendly. I want to make them feel better."

Nurses may do different tests to figure out what is wrong with a patient.

What Other Jobs Might I Like?

Paramedic

Physical therapist

Physician

WHO WORKS WITH NURSES?

Mary works with doctors to give her patients the very best care. Nurses also work with physical therapists, nursing and medical students, and counselors. Nurses work closely with a patient's family. Some nurses help family members care for the patient at home. These nurses are called home health care nurses.

Doctors and nurses work together to give patients the best possible care.

How Might My Job Change?

Some nurses become teachers in nursing schools. Others go back to school and learn more complicated skills. Some nurses with a lot of experience oversee other nurses in hospitals, home care, or nursing homes.

assess (uh-SESS) to find out or decide the importance of a problem

WHEN DO ER NURSES HELP PEOPLE?

Have you ever broken a bone? Someone probably took you to the Emergency Room, or ER. People go to the ER if they have had an accident or need medical help quickly. Nurses in the ER must to be ready to **assess** and care for any medical emergency.

Emergency room nurses often see many people during their work day.

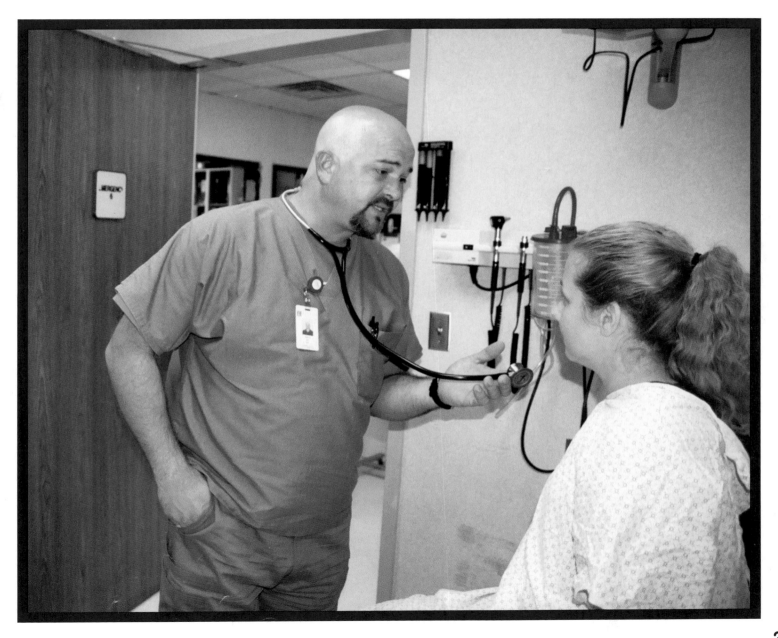

I WANT TO BE A NURSE!

I think being a nurse would be a great way to be a neighborhood helper. Someday I may be the nurse who helps you feel better!

Helping people take care of their bodies is an important job. Maybe one day it will be the job for you!

Is This Job Growing?

The need for nurses will grow more than other jobs.

pulse rate (PUHLSS RAYT) a measurement of how fast someone's heart is beating

WHY DON'T YOU TRY BEING A NURSE?

Do you think you would like to be a nurse? Nurses often measure a person's **pulse rate.**

Try measuring your own pulse rate. Find your pulse by putting two fingers on the palm side of your wrist. Can you feel the blood pumping? Count how many times your pulse beats in one minute. This is your pulse rate. A child's

pulse rate should be 85 to 100 beats per minute.

     Try jumping up and down twenty times. Then take your pulse rate again. Is it lower or higher? What do you think caused a change in your pulse rate?

Nurses take a person's pulse rate to see how fast his or her heart is beating.

HOW TO LEARN MORE
ABOUT NURSES

BOOKS

Brill, Marlene Targ. *Nurses.* Minneapolis: Lerner, 2005.

Flanagan, Alice K., and Christine Osinski (photographer). *Ask Nurse Pfaff, She'll Help You!* Danbury, Conn. Children's Press, 1997.

Robert, James. *Nurses: People Who Care for Our Health.* Vero Beach, Fla.: Rourke Book Company, 1995.

Whitelaw, Nancy. *Clara Barton: Civil War Nurse.* Springfield, N.J.: Enslow, 1997.

WEB SITES

Visit our home page for lots of links about nurses:
http://www.childsworld.com/links

Note to Parents, Teachers, and Librarians:
We routinely check our Web links to make sure they're safe, active sites—so encourage your readers to check them out!

ABOUT THE AUTHORS:

Dr. Cecilia Minden is a university professor and reading specialist with classroom and administrative experience in grades K–12. She is the author of many books for early readers. Cecilia and her husband Dave Cupp live in North Carolina. She earned her PhD in reading education from the University of Virginia.

Linda M. Armantrout received her nurses training at Saint John's School of Nursing in Tulsa, Oklahoma. She has had many opportunities to practice nursing skills with her eight children and nine grandchildren. Linda and her husband Glen live in Louisiana.

INDEX